FEARLESS

How My Journey To Self Love Will Inspire Yours

Stephen Ukaoma

Apex. Achieve Personal Excellence

For God and Emmanuel C.

CONTENTS

INTRODUCTION

#FeelingMyself - 3.2 million Instagram posts of an intangible state of being for which we all strive. Social media and the pursuit of happiness has created a void in our lives we didn't know we needed so desperately to fill. But what if I told you that 3.199 million of those posts weren't representative of true self love. The external approval of your internal self won't fill your void.

I'm Stephen Ukaoma, and I was an addict. Twelve years of self medication led me to a realization that my confidence, arrogance rather, wasn't actually self love and that my void was deeper and darker than anyone knew.

Fueled by my personal pilgrimage toward self love, I was compelled to write this book by the heartfelt confessions of my life coaching clients, *"Stephen, I don't know how to love myself. I don't know what the problem is and I don't know what to do."* Their words echoed familiar feelings.

I'm humbled to share with you my journey. The silver lining of my struggle is this opportunity to provide you with the necessary tools to let go of the past and create a future rich with freedom and self love.

In this book, I'll take you by the hand, sharing pieces of my story, inspiring and motivational self love wisdom along with the EXACT steps, processes and daily routines to release damaging self-talk and negative beliefs, and replace them with love.

We all want to feel good about ourselves, live an amazing life and know how to achieve it. I completely understand. I struggled with this as well, not recognizing the patterns.

This may be your first time dipping your toe into personal growth. Or you have quite possibly already examined plenty of other options as this is far from your first rodeo. Either way, you feel like you're just not where you want to be and are unsure of how to fix it.

Personal experience, research, coupled with consuming every self love book I could get my hands on, I discovered teachings, tools and practices that actually work. In the years that I have been life coaching, I have had the honor and privilege to see my clients truly do the work. Obtaining incredible results. Cultivating lasting and healthy relationships. Pursuing lifelong dreams. Overcoming addiction. Strengthening friendships and family ties. Feeling confident and good about themselves. Feeling truly happy. Achieving Personal Excellence.

The Importance Of Self Love...

#1: Overcome self-doubt and self-defeating thoughts

Cultivating self love truly makes a big difference in the thoughts that jostle for space in your mind. Can you imagine what life would be like if you were able to consistently have loving, nurturing, self-validating thoughts... and when negative ones emerge, you possessed the power to gently make them disappear.

#2: Engage in healthier relationships

You have more than likely heard a number of times that *"You have to love yourself before you can love somebody else."* Even though this may not be completely true, the relationship runs the risk of being severely strained because if we're in self-judgment mode, we have the tendency to unconsciously project our own fears, insecurities, or judgments onto others. If each person within the relationship holds a healthy sense of self love only then can a healthy relationship truly blossom.

#3: Advance your career and have greater financial abundance

What would your life look like if you had a boost in confidence? Would you ask for a promotion or a raise? Would you take greater risks, change careers, or even start your own business? Would you say YES to having more abundance in your life and truly feel worthy of it? In order to have confidence, and to allow the abundance flow in, it takes self love.

#4: Liberate yourself from past pain and suffering

Are you still haunted by your past? Are there people, places, or situations that expel painful memories or negative reactions for you? Do you still denigrate or judge yourself for things you've done? Cultivating a healthy sense of self love means first forgiving yourself and others. It means letting go and knowing that deep down in your heart of hearts, you are worthy... no matter what has transpired in the past.

#5: Be able to possess gratitude as well as peace of mind regardless of any circumstance.

When life gets tough, do you struggle with maintaining a sense of gratitude? By strengthening your self love muscles, you'll develop the ability to discover your truest, highest self and know that all is well, no matter what happens or what you're faced with. Self love helps you to be **FEARLESS**.

So what holds people back from truly loving themselves? There are a bevy of common myths that

people believe which stop them from loving themselves, such as:

- *"I don't know what to do."*
- *"I'm not good enough."*
- *"I've tried this before and it just doesn't work."*
- *"I'm haunted by my past."*
- *"I have to achieve something in order to be worthy of love."*
- *"Nobody knows me and if they did, they wouldn't love me either."*
- *"I had a horrible childhood and I'll never get out from under it."*
- *"I never felt loved unconditionally. How can I love myself?"*
- *"I'm not worthy of love or anything good."*
- *"I'd feel better if I… (had a partner, had a better job, had more money, was more attractive, was more accomplished…)"*
- *"I don't really matter."*

But it doesn't have to be this way at all. Eradicating those myths, first requires making the choice to believe that loving yourself and living a fulfilling life is in fact possible. Then, when you take conscious, inspired and committed action to completely love yourself, that is when you erase those myths.

Imagine yourself waking up in the morning in a state of complete gratitude and knowing you matter, that you are truly worthy and loved. You get dressed feeling good about the way you look. You head to work feeling powerful and confident. You relate to everyone in a way that is authentic and brings out their best. You boldly take risks and you assertively express yourself as well as your dreams. You no longer base your behavior or worth according to what other people may think of you.

Imagine that you have more empowering things to say about yourself than condescending. Your natural way is to always be compassionate and respectful of yourself. And you keep your arms wide open to receive all the abundance, because you now know you deserve it. You can go to sleep at night knowing that you are living a life that you're truly fired up about, and you love yourself just the way you are. How will this impact you?

Now, this may be pretty close to the life you live now, and you're just a few minor adjustments away. Or it might be so far fetched from anything you've experienced, you're thinking... How can this work for me?

Well, I can tell you this,

Can I guarantee that you'll be a brand new person after the completion of this book? No, I can't and I won't. That would be a pretty dishonest and an irresponsible claim to make, in my opinion.

However...

I can and will give you a process as well as a means

to cultivate profound, long lasting self love. In this book, I will set everything out in an organized and very easy to follow way, and I'll walk you through every step. You'll get self love teachings and specific self love tools, exercises, and practices to help elevate your self love to levels you never dreamed of.

I wrote this book to be different from other books. A lot of people say *"you just have to love yourself,"* but they don't tell you how. I continually heard this complaint, so I wrote this book to tackle the *"how"* in a clear, simple, and most effective way possible. I've done all the *"figuring it out"* so you do not have to.

You'll reap the benefits of my blood, sweat and tears. I've developed an exact step-by-step system. No fluffy concepts you can't put into use. No *"good luck, see ya later."* and even though I know you're smart and highly capable, I'll be there with you EVERY SINGLE STEP of the way and guide you through EXACTLY what to do.

SELF LOVE
JUMP START

What Is Self-Love?

Self love. Quite the buzz word these days. It sounds amazing and desirable, but what does it actually mean? How do we love ourselves and why does it matter?

Self love is complete acceptance while treating yourself with kindness and respect; cultivating your growth and well-being.

Self love encompasses not only how you treat yourself, but also your thoughts and feelings, your self talk. Understanding the concept of self love, shifts your mindset toward compassion and care instead of disappointment and uncertainty. Imagine how you can feel, treat and speak to yourself differently.

Loving yourself forges a positive view of yourself. This doesn't mean you feel positive about yourself all the time. That is unrealistic! It's completely natural to temporarily feel upset, angry, or disappointed with yourself and still love yourself. If this seems difficult to grasp, think about how this works in other relationships. For example, I can love my brother even though I sometimes feel angry or disappointed with him. Even in the midst of my anger and disappointment, my love for him informs how I relate to him. It allows me to forgive him, consider his feelings, meet his needs, and make decisions that will support his well-being. Self love is very much the same. Which means, if you know how to love others, you know how to love yourself.

What Does Self Love Actually Look Like?

The following are examples of how self love looks in action:

- *Positive Affirmations*
- *Forgiving yourself when you make mistakes*
- *Self Care- Assessing and Meeting your needs above others*
- *Being more assertive*
- *Not allowing others take advantage of you or abuse you*
- *Prioritizing your health and wellness*
- *Surrounding yourself with people who support you and build you up (avoiding those who do not)*
- *Asking for help*
- *Relinquishing grudges or anger that hold you back*
- *Recognizing your strengths*

- *Valuing your feelings*
- *Making healthy choices majority of the time*
- *Living according to your values*
- *Pursuing your goals and interests*
- *Challenging yourself*
- *Holding yourself accountable*
- *Giving yourself healthy rewards*
- *Accepting your flaws and imperfections*
- *Setting realistic expectations*
- *Noticing and rewarding your progress and effort*

Why Is This Important?

If you grew up without a significant role model of self love, without clear guidance of the importance of being good to yourself, you might question its value. Without self love, you are highly predisposed to self-criticism and can easily fall victim to people pleasing and perfectionism. You're also more likely to tolerate abuse or mistreatment from others. By not valuing yourself, you may neglect your needs and feelings. Self sabotage or making poor decisions that aren't in your best interest can be soon to follow.

Self love truly is the foundation that allows us to be more assertive, set boundaries, and cultivate healthy relationships with others. Practicing self-care, pursuing our interests and goals, and feeling proud of who we truly are is how we get there.

Self Love And Narcissism

I'm sure you find yourself questioning whether self love is really necessary. A huge barrier to self love is the notion that it's narcissistic or self-centered. Societal pressures suggest being too confident or arrogant is a negative trait, especially for women. It's considered bad manners to gloat or boast about one's accomplishments. Women often try to take up the least amount of physical space as possible in public situations, feeling undeserving or not wanting to be seen as entitled.

When psychologists and even therapists encourage self love, it's not about putting yourself on a pedestal. Narcissists lack empathy. They believe they're better than others, not acknowledging or taking responsibility for their actions and flaws. They also seek extreme amounts of external validation and recognition.

Self love, on the other hand, isn't about showing off how wonderful you are. People who love themselves in a healthy manner understand that they are flawed, make mistakes, and they accept and care about themselves in spite of their imperfections. Self love doesn't stop you from caring about others; it simply means you can give yourself the same kindness that you give to others.

Jump Start Your Self Love And Put It Into Practice

When things are hard to do, we typically avoid them. Let's start by avoiding thoughts like these:

- *I'll take a break and focus on myself after I've taken care of my family.*
- *Acknowledging my feelings and journaling sounds like a lot of work.*
- *I'm afraid I won't be able to change.*
- *I want to be less self-critical, but I don't know how.*
- *Self-care seems self-indulgent.*
- *I have way too much to do.*
- *I know this relationship isn't good for me, but I don't want to be alone.*
- *I've been making it on five hours of sleep for years, so it can't be that bad.*

It's normal to be overwhelmed or even ambivalent about self love or making any kind of change. However, loving yourself doesn't mean you have to change everything about your life. You'll simply treat yourself a little better than you did yesterday.

Let's get started, shall we? I invite you to identify one loving thing you can do for yourself today. It could be a positive thought or action. Next, write down your action and your due date. Committing to yourself in writing is important to increase accountability and make it more likely that you'll follow through. As you add more and more loving thoughts and actions to your daily life, they'll grow into habits, while forcing out your self-defeating thoughts and behaviors. Keep it up, with practice, self love will become second nature.

ACTION ITEM: Write down one loving thing you can do for yourself along with the due date. Add the due date to your calendar, preferably to your phone. Share with a friend or relative to help keep you accountable.

LETTER TO MY FATHER

December 15, 2019: 9:35 a.m.

Dear Dad,

How are you? Hope all is well with you. I wanted to reach out to you because I am very much saddened about our estranged relationship... I know that it is my fault. Back in 2005, when I first came to North Carolina, I was beyond happy and grateful, not only for a new fresh start but to finally cultivate a relationship with my father... the man that I strived to emulate... as imitation is the highest form of flattery. I remember the long father and son talks we had when you would speak to me about what to expect in life and how to be a man. I still value those talks till this very day. The book that you gave me... "A Purpose Driven Life By Rick Warren" is by far one of the best gifts I've been given... and the words from that book still hold dear to my heart.

Dad, I just want you to know that I truly do appreciate all that you have done for me because I know that you truly meant well and wanted me to be well as your first son. When you received me in 2005, I was a lost and a mentally immature boy in a man's body... I had a skewed perception of life and at that time... anything good that you tried to do for me or anything good that would come to me, I would self sabotage it inexplicably. I struggled with feeling love, worthiness, and had a litany of inadequacies that I had no answer for. I was broken and felt as though I had no identity... I didn't know whether I was coming or going... I had no direction. I turned to alcohol and drugs to ease the pain that was killing me from the inside out... something that I never thought in my life I'd become, I became... I was a full blown drug addict. I hid my addiction from everyone... including you. But deep down I was screaming loudly for help. You were there for me in the midst of my self induced calamities... but you had no way of knowing the true depths of my despair. DUI after DUI... reckless days and nights... on and off drugs... I couldn't help myself... no one could.

I have since gotten my life back on track with hard work in terms of truly facing my demons that plagued me internally, and by the grace of God. I just want you to know that none of this is your fault... and that all that you tried to do for me was coming from a good place... a place of a father that loves his son. I wasn't in the right state of mind to receive the love that you tried to give me due to my immaturity as well as my deep seeded issues that I kept secluded from you.

You are my father that I love, respect, and truly revere. I am not seeking anything from you other than a relationship with my father... I miss my father, I need my father... I am of you and without you... I am not a whole man. Every son needs his father... and this is no different. I am asking as humbly as I know how to please forgive me for my past transgressions and let us take the first steps in rectifying our bond... as father and son. All I need is an opportunity... I can show you better than I can tell you. May God open your heart to receive me...

Sincerely your Son,
Stephen

THE LINCOLN: ACCEPTANCE

It's a bone chilling night on October 17, 2018 in San Francisco. It's 3:13 a.m. and I'm sitting in my '98 Lincoln Continental outside of Wells Fargo on Lombard and Fillmore. The Lincoln had been my home for the previous two weeks, and it showed. A cascade of 24oz cans of Olde English Malt liquor adorned my back seat, like "*I tried my best*" ribbons, for not resorting to the hard stuff. The reality was, that was just my attempt to level myself out from the high. It is possible to get "*too high.*" Going on 46 hours of being awake can prove it.

My gas tank is on E. I'm feeling trapped in what was once my source of pride and accomplishment, but is now my coffin of regret. My crack pipe is on the passenger floorboard after my fifth attempt to cast it aside and go to sleep. Yet my meth pipe remains in my hand. I'm paranoid, cold, hungry, and fearing the imminent comedown. As I relentlessly flick my lighter to get another hit, I question myself; *How did it get this far? Why am I doing this to myself? Is this the way my life plays out?*

Damn, my lighter is out of fluid... my car is out of gas and I'm out of options.

I desperately needed another hit to drown out my emotions, my pain, and the ongoing monologue of paranoia and the plotting with Satan in my mind. Being a black man in the Marina (an upper class neighborhood in SF) smoking meth inside my car had me flinching to look over my shoulder at any peripheral movement. *What if that woman calls the police? Can that man see the flame of the lighter through my tinted windows? Can they hear my thoughts?*

I had seven dollars in my posession. The yield of my most recent acquaintance manipulation. *"Hey man, I just need twenty bucks if you can spot me, I really appreciate it."* No one suspected my double life.

In between binges, I managed to drag myself to the gym. Part vanity, part sanity, it kept me moving forward at the very least. More importantly, it kept up appearances.

I rationalized that I could spend a buck or two on a new lighter, to get this much needed last hit. I glanced about the horizon and made the exit from my safe zone - the Lincoln. Walking briskly to the nearest gas station, I kept my eyes steady ahead of me. You're already a target being black, especially walking at night. I exchanged my hard earned cash for liquid peace of mind and quickly returned to the safety of my vehicle. The cover of the night and the tint of my windows gave me a false sense of security. With a renewed sense of purpose, I lit up my meth pipe with the vigor of a triathlete zipping up his wetsuit. However, no matter how hard I tried, the dragon had fled. Sleep deprived and emotionally broken, my body gave up my fight with the meth and I fell asleep.

Self Acceptance starts with a first step. This was the night before mine.

You'll never be able to create the right reality if you aren't willing to let the wrong one go.

"A journey of a thousand miles begins with a single step." So said ancient Chinese philosopher, Lao Tzu.

The first step to changing your life is acknowledging and accepting where you are right now. Putting your head in the sand just doesn't cut it when it comes to change. When you begin to face and accept where you are in life, you are giving yourself the power to change it. Look at your pain and admit what you don't like.

You won't be able to take sustainable steps towards change until you look plainly at where you are. Breathe it in, deeply. Know that your choices got you to this point and your choices will get you out. This is where acceptance comes into play and this is the first step.

In Deepak's Chopra's The Seven Laws Of Spiritual Success, law number four - The Law of Least Effort - states, *"Accept people, situations, and events as they occur. Take responsibility for your situation and for all events seen as problems. Relinquish the need to defend your point of view."*

We need to receive with open arms what happens to us, because if we fight and resist it, we are creating a lot of turbulence in our minds. He further explains that if we want things to be different in the future, we need to accept things as they are in the present moment.

How To Live A Life Free Of Limiting Beliefs

The next morning I jolted awake with the sun indiscriminately judging my night's transgressions. Although the orange hue bathed my current reality, I was frozen from head to toe. I didn't have much time to register the near freezing degrees, which had begun to swell my feet. The hunger pangs set in so fierce that I thought I might pass out. *How long has it been since I ate?* Not an unfamiliar sentiment when you're wired for days on end. I'm familiar with this neighborhood, I live here. But I haven't been in this dire need of sustenance this early in the morning. God was looking out for me this morning. Mel's Diner, like an oasis in the desert, was open across the street. I counted and recounted my five dollars as if

I had missed some magical windfall of cash whilst sleeping in my own arctic tundra. I knew it wasn't enough. I also knew, I didn't care.

I sheepishly requested the next available diner booth. Typically I would be overly concerned with my appearance, my aesthetics as well as my position in the restaurant (the narcissist in me). This morning my mission did not consider personal entitlements nor human decencies. I needed food, and I wasn't above begging, borrowing, or stealing.

I ordered a short stack of pancakes. Still rather reasonable considering my state of mind. I ate those pancakes like I was surrounded by a pack of wild dogs, all vying for my take. Anxiety set in as the waitress left the check on my table and told me it was *"no hurry."* No matter how many times I recounted my five dollars, it still wasn't enough. The decision had already been made, I just now had to carry it out. Leave what I had. Walk out. That's what I did.

I ambled back to my safe zone - the Lincoln, my feet blistering from the cold and neglect. As I hunkered down in my car, I could smell myself and it was making me feel nauseated. The end of the line was here. As much as I had put it off, I knew my only next step had to be rehab.

I had managed to pull myself together and check into a rehab facility known as The Delancey Street Foundation. I had come into their care a broken man and thought I could trust this process.

Later that evening, I was led to a dimly lit room within the facility, filled with chairs formed in the shape of a circle. I literally had no idea what to expect. Extremely fatigued, bewildered, and detoxing from the drugs, I found myself surrounded by strangers from all walks of life on the same quest as I.

Out of nowhere, people began shouting obscenities at one another. I was taken aback as to what was going on. They called it a *"game"* but this madness was far from a game. I began to sink further and further in my chair, as if to make myself smaller, hoping that I could avoid being the next victim in the crosshairs of a verbal onslaught. The shouting subsided and my fear came to fruition as a guy called out to me, asking of my story. This was a trap and I felt there was no way out.

I reluctantly started from the beginning. The beginning was a life on the come up. I elaborated about tales of my accomplishments, my beloved Lincoln, the passing of my Real Estate Exam, and moving out of my hometown of Modesto. Abruptly, the man scouted at me, *"Fuck your accomplishments! and fuck what you had! You ain't nothing but a fucking dope fiend!"* Overcome with rage, I shot out of my seat and rushed towards him. The end goal was certain. Transfer my pain, anguish, humiliation, and rage through my fists onto his face.

Several arms reached out to restrain me. As I struggled to break free, I yelled, *"How are you all gonna let him disrespect me like that!?"* Disrespect in my frame of reference was a punishable offense. I was immediately escorted out of the *"game room"* and taken outside to the balcony which overlooked the Bay Bridge to cool off and get some fresh air. The Foundation has a zero tolerance for violence. I was given a stern warning that night.

The *"Games"* took place four nights a week. It's a platform that's provided in whereby you can honestly say how you feel about someone in hopes of bringing about change, blowing off steam, or simply putting others down and crushing their self esteem. The intent of the *"Games"* was an attack therapy approach for behavior modification. The reality of it was a room full of 15-20 convicts, drug addicts, and felons screaming negativity and antagonizing put downs for two hours non stop.
The result of it was it hard wired my previously ingrained limiting beliefs. Proof I was nothing but a dope fiend. Night after night, I was subjected to harsh criticism and putdowns within the confines of the *"Games."* How could you roll the dice with someone's psyche? The games were taking its toll on my state of mind as they continued to send me into a deeper mental depression.
"Your girlfriend doesn't fucking love you. She's out there fucking some other dude right now".
"You are a manipulative snake"
"Stupid muthafucka"

"Bitch"
"Dope fiend"
"Crackhead"
"You're soft" - This was the worst. Maybe I believed it too much. And the deprecating monologue went on and on as I replayed the tape of the horrible things that were uttered to me.

I had two options, break under the pressure, or get thicker skin. God was putting me through trial by fire and I was singed. I was paying for all my narcissistic ways coupled with my addiction. I was now forced to be present through the pain without the numbing effects of crack cocaine, meth, or alcohol.

The hard reality for many of us is that we're so crippled by the burden of limiting beliefs we develop through our lives, that we do not have the confidence to take that first and all important step. How many potential life changing opportunities have passed you by because you're convinced that you just don't measure up?

"I'm not smart enough", or *"I don't have the right physical attributes or cultural background..."*

And so our inner monologue cycles on repeat. In reality, whether or not it's true, it becomes your truth. Remember, *"It's not who you are that holds you back, it's who you think you're not."*

One of the most damaging of all human characteristics is self-doubt, also known as limiting beliefs.

Doubting your own abilities or worthiness quickly leads to a whole slew of limiting beliefs which are ultimately self-fulfilling.

As Henry Ford famously said: *"Whether you think you can, or think you can't, you're right."* Allow yourself to believe that you can't do something, it's a certainty you will fail. So, how can we eradicate these self-limiting beliefs and boldly step forward into a bright future where the sky is truly the limit?

Step By Step I'll Tell You...

Step 1: Write down your limiting belief.

Be your own detective. Follow your thoughts and emotions to find the limiting beliefs that are holding you back. Stare them in the face. You may want to note how strong each belief is and what emotions they elicit within you.

Step 2: Acknowledge that these are simply beliefs, not real truths

In many cases, this is the hardest step. *"But, my limitations are real!"* This is where the power of choice comes in. What are you more interested in: defending your limitations to the bitter death or achieving your goals and desires? The author Evelyn Waugh wrote, *"When we argue for our limitations, we get to keep them."* The choice is yours and the power is in your hands.

Step 3: Challenge the limiting belief with a new belief

Create a belief that is in line with what you want. For example, *"My financial hardships in the past have taught me so much that I'm better prepared to handle them now!"* Or, *"Having prevailed over being in an unhealthy and toxic relationship, I've learned what to look for in a happy, and loving significant other!"*

The key is to go beyond just saying it. You want to really BECOME this new belief. Create that new mindset. Experience how it feels to live your new truth. If done wholeheartedly, Steps 2 and 3 will go a long way to the destruction of your limiting beliefs.

Step 4: Take action

This may feel scary, but you must act as if your new belief is true. For example, if you are the kind of confident man that women adore; how are you conducting yourself at a social gathering? Who are you chatting up or asking out? You have really learned a lot from past financial hardships; what steps are you taking to ensure a lucrative future? You really are the kind of person who eats healthy food; which whole foods are you adding to your grocery cart?

If you shy away from taking any steps based on your new belief, you will only feed your old limiting belief and continue to repeat the same, self defeating cycle. Taking action, even the smallest of steps, will help solidify your new unlimited mindset. Your first steps do not have to be perfect, but they must be headed in the right direction. And remember, be sure to acknowledge yourself when you've taken that step. This is critical.

Now that we have the steps down to combat limiting beliefs… we must now begin to embrace our self worth and in doing this opens us up for more loving and compatible relationships. Knowing our worth is paramount.

One of the keys to be able to reach our goals and face life with more poise is to be aware of our worthiness. When we are conscious about our self worth, we are in a better position to gain happiness from life, and our ability to cope with whatever life brings is greatly increased. The question now is, how we can be more conscious of our self worth?

Step 1: Provide Value and You Will Feel Valuable

The first and best way to greatly improve your feelings of worthiness is simply to provide value to others. Practice being kind to others as well as to yourself. Truly be of service. This means providing value with no expectations of receiving anything in return. The requirement is that you give unconditionally. Giving with expectation, is trading and not real giving. It's highly difficult to manifest what you want without being of service to others. Providing value through being of service to others, creates a void that the universe will fill for you. What you put out, you shall receive. Providing value to others in turn will make you feel valuable.

Step 2: Keep Your Promises

A crucial part of being of service that at times gets overlooked is keeping promises that you make to yourself, as well as what you promise to others. Learning to live up to your promises inevitably builds trust from others, and increases confidence within yourself. This will lead to a better perspective of your worth. When you set achievable goals and put in place plans to meet them, you will truly experience a much higher rate of success and this will drive up your worthiness. You need to make goal setting (and promise keeping) a consistent, persistent behavior, which will then allow you to embrace the pursuit of your full potential by creating objectives and accomplishing them.

Step 3: Accountability Is Knowing You Are Worthy

Having accountability is another way to improve your feelings of self worth. Accountability gives you the power and control over everything in your life. Accountability truly means that you don't live in a world of blame, shame, or justification. Instead, you take on all challenges as an opportunity to learn and grow. People who are accountable ask themselves two important questions when challenges arise:

- *What did I do to attract it to myself?*
- *What am I supposed to learn from it?*

The tendency of people to go *"below the line"* comes from the impulse to defend their pride and ego. But in all actuality, they are avoiding accountability. Going below the line is a sure fire way to lower your self worthiness. It's good to invite others to help keep you accountable. Whether it's a spouse, a co-worker, or a coach, ask them to make sure that you stay on track with achieving your goals. If you are unable to find anyone that you trust, then you may keep track of your words and actions yourself. Journaling is a very effective way to do this. Be sure to be completely honest with your evaluation of your performance.

Step 4: Continue To Raise The Bar

If you want to make a long lasting improvement to your self-image and raise your worthiness, you must embrace the principles of service, keep promises you make to yourself (as well as to others), set realistic goals that you can achieve, and CONTINUE to keep raising the bar. Finally, take charge of your life by being accountable and living above the line of blame, shame, and justification.

These strategies are well worth your time and to your benefit, if you want to build your self worth, feel like you are deserving, and consistently, persistently, rapidly attract the great things that are coming your way.

Now that we have covered the two critical parts of acceptance, lastly, it's time to go over how to open your heart to love and embrace yourself...

Opening Yourself To Love And Embracing Yourself

We often close ourselves off when traumatic events happen in our lives. Instead of allowing the world to soften us, we let it drive us deeper into ourselves. We try to deflect the hurt and pain by pretending it doesn't exist. Although we can try this all we want, in the end, we cannot hide from ourselves. We need to learn to open our hearts to the potentials of life and allow the world to soften us.
Whenever you start to let your fears and serious-ness get the best of you, it's best to take a step back and reevaluate your behavior.

ACTION ITEM: Thoroughly identify and write down all of your limiting beliefs. This will be your starting point to eradicating damaging negative self talk. Now rewrite each limiting belief in the affirm-ative.

Example:

Limiting Belief - *"I'm not strong enough to raise my*

children alone."
Affirmative Belief - *"I'm strong enough to raise my children alone."*

DELANCEY STREET: SELF FORGIVENESS

Daydreaming about my past and what led me to this point in my life in which I found myself in a rehab facility, I began to reminisce about the time prior to my arrival to rehab when I had seen the glossy brochures as well as the dated promo video online about Delancey Street. My addiction at that time was lying dormant within me as I was struggling to pick up the pieces from the last binge about a month and a half before. I knew that I needed to get help, but I was unwilling to concede to the help of rehab and this included Delancey Street. To say I was disinterested was an understatement. I believed I could do it on my own, as that's what my pride led me to believe.

Listening to my pride failed me yet again which ultimately led me to another self induced drug and alcohol binge. I had completely sabotaged everything good that had been restored to me and based upon my poor choices and lack of better judgment, I now found myself staring at the white walls and stark decor filled with the president and CEO of Delancey Street. I'm seeing less "rehab resort" and more JonesTown. I cried and cried every day, continually beating myself up for what I had done to my life, and to those who were close to me. I couldn't seem to forgive myself for what I had done. I was in mental purgatory.

I would isolate from the other residents as much as I possibly could to be in my head as it was my only escape from the present reality. I would sit on the balcony and gaze at the water's edge from the Embarcadero. Tears stained my cheeks as I strained to see the Bay Bridge. A long time resident at the program approached to check on me. Noticing my grief, he paused from his chores and gave me some advice which became invaluable in my upcoming journey. My ongoing monologue of the wrong I had done was finally coming to its last act.

We often hear a lot about the importance of forgiving those who have wronged us, but what about the importance of forgiving ourselves? Isn't that important as well? I believe wholeheartedly that it is.

When we harm someone it is normal and healthy to feel badly about it, to experience deep regret and to wish we could take it back or do something to make the person feel better. What is unhealthy is to continually beat ourselves up for our transgressions and to draw the conclusion that we are a bad person as a result of it. The first experience is generally thought of as guilt the second is known as shame.

Shame and guilt can feel very similar and in both emotions we truly feel bad about ourselves. **Guilt**, can be best understood as feeling disappointed in oneself for violating an important moral value or behavior. Feeling guilty can in fact be healthy. It can lead to positive behavior change. With **shame**, one can also feel a disappointment in oneself but no real value has been violated.

Shame is very unhealthy, causing lowered self-esteem, and feelings of unworthiness. It can truly be a debilitating emotion. Shame is responsible for a litany of problems, such as:

- *Self criticism and self blame*
- *Self neglect*
- *Self destructive behaviors (abusing your body with food, alcohol, drugs, cigarettes, etc)*
- *Self sabotaging behavior (starting fights with loved ones, sabotaging jobs, etc)*
- *The belief that you do not deserve good things*
- *Intense rage (frequent physical fights, road rage)*
- *Acting out against society (breaking the rules, breaking the law)*
- *Continuing to repeat the cycle of abuse through either victim behavior or abusive behavior*

The difference between shame and guilt can be best defined as such, when we feel guilty, we feel bad about something we did or failed to carry out. But when we feel shame, we feel bad about who we are. When we feel guilt, we need to learn and understand that it is okay to make mistakes. And when we feel shame we need to learn that it is okay to be who we are.

Self forgiveness is the most powerful step you can take to free yourself of debilitating shame. This is especially true for those who have been abused; however, it applies to everyone. Self forgiveness is absolutely essential if we want to become emotionally healthy and have a peace of mind. The more shame you heal, the more you will be able to see yourself more clearly, the good as well as the bad. You will be able to recognize and admit how you have harmed yourself and others. Your relationships with others will change and deepen exponentially. More importantly, your relationship with yourself will greatly improve.

There are four avenues that lead toward self forgiveness, and as difficult as it may seem to be able to forgive yourself for the harm you have caused others, there are several effective ways to go about it:

1. *Self-understanding*
2. *Common humanity*
3. *Earning your Forgiveness: taking responsibility, apologizing and making amends*

4. Asking your higher power for forgiveness

Self-Understanding Can Lead You To Self Forgiveness

Understanding that the trauma you endured created problems within you that were out of your control, can go a long way towards forgiving yourself for the ways that you have hurt others. For example, understanding that your addiction whether it was to drugs, alcohol, sex, porn, food, shopping, gambling, etc, was a way to self medicate and to cope with anxiety and fear, can help you to stop mentally beating yourself up for the harm your addiction caused to those close to you. Understanding that the reason you have become abusive or have developed a pattern of allowing others to abuse you comes directly from your abusive experiences, and this will hopefully help you to stop chastising yourself for these behaviors.

Common Humanity

The recognition of **common humanity** allows us to be more understanding and less judgmental about our inadequacies. Our thoughts, feelings and actions are impacted in large part by factors outside of our control such as our upbringing, culture, genetic and environmental conditions, as well as the demands and expectations of others. If we truly had full control over our behavior, how many people would consciously choose to have anger issues, an addiction, crippling social anxiety, an eating disorder? When you examine your mistakes and failures it becomes clear that you did not consciously choose to make them and even in those rare cases when you did make a conscious choice, the motivation for your actions was colored by your abuse or other experiences. Because of the shame you have carried, you closed your heart to others and became blind to how your actions were harming others.

Many aspects of ourselves as well as the circumstances of our lives are not of our intentional choosing, but they derive from a litany of factors that are outside our sphere of influence. When we acknowledge this reality, failings and life difficulties do not have to be taken so personally.

Getting closer to Self Forgiveness

Now that you have a better understanding of common humanity, it's time to exercise those sins and omissions.

Write a list of the people you have harmed and how you have harmed them. One by one, go through your list and write down the causes as well as the conditions that led you to this action or lack thereof. You've already made the connection between your harmful actions and the fact that you were abused or neglected. Now think of other major factors such as a family history of violence and a family history of addiction, as well as more subtle factors such as stress due to financial problems or marital problems.

Now ask yourself to consider why you did not stop yourself from harming this person. For example, were you so full of rage that you couldn't control yourself? Did you hate yourself so much that you didn't care how much you hurt someone else? Had you built up such a defensive wall that you couldn't have empathy or compassion for the person you harmed?

Now that you have a better understanding of the causes and conditions that led you to act in the way that you did, try to apply the concept of Common Humanity toward yourself. You were an imperfect, fallible human being and like all humans sometimes do, you acted in ways that hurt someone else. Honor the limitations of your human imperfections and have compassion for yourself. Forgive yourself.

Earning Your Forgiveness

If you continue to find difficulties forgiving yourself, ask yourself this one important question: *"Why wouldn't I want to forgive myself?"* If your answer is *"I don't deserve it,"* that is truly your shame talking. If you feel like you don't deserve forgiveness, perhaps you may need to earn it.

So how do you earn forgiveness? First and foremost,

you need to truly admit to yourself as well as others the wrongs you have committed. Unless you tell the full truth about how you harmed others, but first to yourself and then to the person or people you have hurt (if possible), you may not believe that you deserve to be forgiven. (And on the flip side, unless you admit what you did to harm the person or people you that you have harmed, they may not be willing to forgive you.)

Dwelling on your transgressions does no one any good, and this includes the person you harmed.

When you accept responsibility for your actions you may feel more shame; however, that feeling of shame will be replaced with a feeling of self respect and of genuine pride (as opposed to false pride).

The best way to prepare yourself for this process goes something like this:

Spend some quiet time thinking honestly and deeply about how your actions have harmed the person.
The following sentence may help in this process:
"I harmed _________ by ____________________."
Next, write down all the ways your action harmed this person.
"I caused _______________ to suffer in the following ways _______________."

After you've done the first two steps, you need to go to those you have harmed and admit what you have done to hurt them. It is incumbent upon you that you tell those you have harmed that they have a right to their anger and that you encourage them to voice it directly to you. Keep in mind, that you do not allow anyone to verbally abuse you or to shame you. Taking responsibility may also include admitting to others, such as other family members, how you abused or neglected your victim.

Apologizing Sincerely

Your admittance of what you did to harm others is incredibly powerful if it is accompanied by a heartfelt and sincere apology.

One of the most frequent comments that I hear from those who were abused in a situation is that they wish the offender would admit what he or she did and apologize to them for it. Think back to an incident when you truly felt wronged by another person. What did you want from that person in order to forgive him or her? Most people say they want an apology. Why is this the case? It's not solely the words of, *"I'm sorry"* that we need to hear but we need the wrongdoer to take responsibility for his or her actions and we need to know that the wrongdoer feels regret or remorse for having wronged us.

An apology can remove the cloud of shame that even the most remorseful individual carries around. On the other hand, if you don't experience enough shame when you wrong someone else, an apology can help remind you of the harm you caused. The act of having to apologize to someone usually causes us to feel humiliated. Remembering that humiliation the next time you are tempted to repeat the same act can deter you from acting on impulse.

When we are able to muster up the courage to admit when we are wrong and to work past our fears and resistance to apologize, we cultivate a deep sense of respect within ourselves. This self respect can affect our self esteem, self confidence, as well as our overall outlook on life. When you apologize to someone, you show care and respect for the other person's feelings. You also let the person know that you did not intend to hurt them and that it is your intention to treat them fairly in the future. If you apologize for your wrongdoing, you will not only validate his or her experience but help the person to stop blaming themself for the abuse.

How To Give A Meaningful Apology

A **meaningful apology** is one that communicates what I like to call the three R's: Regret, Responsibility, and Rectification.

> 1. *A statement of regret for having caused the distrust, hurt, or damage. This entails, an expression of deep empathy toward the other person portraying that you understand how your actions caused harm.*

2. *An acceptance of responsibility for your actions. For an apology to be effective, it has be clear that you are accepting complete responsibility for your actions. This means not blaming anyone else for what you did and certainly not making excuses for your actions.*

3. *A statement of your willingness to take some action to rectify the situation. While you cannot go back in time and undo the past, you can, however, do everything within your power to repair the harm you caused. A truly meaningful apology needs to include a statement in which you offer restitution in some manner, an offer to help the other person, or a promise to take action so that you will not repeat the behavior. In the case of emotional or physical abuse, you can go to counseling or a support group to ensure you do not abuse anyone again. You can offer to pay for your victim's therapy or you can donate your time or money to organizations that work to help victims of abuse.*

Ask Your Higher Power For Forgiveness

When we face the truth wholeheartedly about how we have hurt others, the feelings of guilt and shame can be overwhelming. Sometimes, the only way we can find self forgiveness is to reach out to something bigger than ourselves.

Whatever your religious or spiritual beliefs are,

asking your higher power for comfort, compassion, and forgiveness can be a very powerful step in forgiving yourself. This may be as simple as praying to God to forgive you for your sins. You may pray to your higher power for help in the process of self-forgiveness. Many of my clients have stated that by doing this they believe they received help in this endeavor. If you have truly learned from your mistake, and do not wish to repeat it, then you don't need to feel guilty or shameful about it any longer. Forgive yourself, let it go, and move on.

If you find you are still burdened with guilt or shame about how your past behavior has affected someone, it will be very important to know this truth: The most effective way of self forgiveness is for you to vow that you will not continue the same behavior and not hurt someone in the same way ever again.

Acknowledging the interconnected nature of our lives is another important aspect of Common Humanity. The truth is, who we are, how we think, and how we behave is inextricably interwoven with other people and events. In other words, you didn't get to where you are today all by yourself. Your tendency to be a victim or your tendency to be abusive did not just happen. You must continue to look for the causes and conditions that lead you to these unhealthy behavior patterns.

When you examine your mistakes and failures, it

becomes clear that you did not consciously choose to make them and even in those rare cases when you did make a conscious choice, the motivation for your actions was colored by your abuse or other experiences. Because of the shame you have carried, you closed your heart to others and became blind to how your actions were harming others.

We all have harmed others. In fact, every single person in our world has harmed at least one other person in ways that have shaped that person's life. In knowing this and knowing that you are not alone, this can help you to have compassion for yourself and to forgive yourself. Feeling compassion for yourself does not release you from taking responsibility for your actions, but it can truly release you from the self hatred that stymies you from forgiving yourself and free you to respond to the situation with more clarity.

ACTION ITEM: Spend some quiet time thinking honestly and deeply about how your actions have harmed the person.

The following sentence may help in this process:
"I harmed _________ by _____________________."
Next, write down all the ways your action harmed this person.
"I caused_______________ to suffer in the following ways_______________."

Work on your sincere apology to each person you have wronged.

EMMANUEL: SELF COMPASSION

Forgiving myself proved to be a solid foundation I could build upon. I was starting to form strong bonds despite my daily negative surroundings. This led me to my new found best friend, Emmanuel (a fellow Delancey Street resident). True to his biblical name, we embarked upon the deepest spiritual adventure I'd ever dared. We shared our respective journeys, things we had never shared with another living soul. It's rare to find a confidant like this and I relished every moment. The purging of our baggage enabled me to find a new perspective of myself and my situation. I realized that the compassion Emmanuel and I gifted each other, was the same compassion I needed to gift myself. I didn't have to carry around the weight of my sordid past. Nor did I have to be judged by it. I could give it to God, and let it go.

Self compassion is a positive attitude that we have towards ourselves. Having self compassion means being able to understand yourself in a way that is forgiving, accepting, and loving when situations may be less than favorable. We know that it's similar to self love and that it's distinct from self esteem.

Self kindness is about showing kindness and understanding toward ourselves when we fail at something, or when we feel emotion. Instead of being critical or judging ourselves harshly when we already are in pain, we can learn to see the negative influence of self judgment and treat ourselves with love and patience.
In a nutshell, showing self kindness means treating our worth unconditionally even when we fall short of our own expectations, whether it's through our thoughts or actions.

We also see a lot of key themes popping up that you may already be very familiar with, such as, empathy, kindness, forgiveness, caring, and a bevy of synonyms for acceptance and non judgment. So much of our mental activity is ingrained or instinctual, it can take a conscious effort at first to start practicing self compassion.

How To Show Yourself Self Compassion:

Treat Yourself As You'd Treat A Friend

A good place to start is by thinking about how you would treat those that you care about. Although we cannot always take away the hurt and pain of others, we can acknowledge its existence and provide support to help them get through it and grow. Be easy on yourself as you are human, allow yourself to make mistakes and when you do, don't beat yourself up for it. This is truly about being understanding and empathetic towards yourself. For example, If a friend is feeling down, hurt, or upset, you might physically pat them on the back or hold their hand. This is how you treat yourself in times of failure and despair.

Becoming More Self Aware

Becoming more aware of our internal narratives is a positive starting point for changing our self talk.

Use *"Releasing Statements."* Maybe you're not a fan of positive affirmations. Maybe they don't feel natural or you believe they don't quite reach you on a subconscious level. If this so happens to be the case, then you may want to try using a technique called *"Releasing Statements."* For example, when you catch yourself thinking a negative thought such as *"I'm such a mean and horrible person for getting upset."* in this moment try turning it around and *"releasing"* yourself from the feeling. Instead, say to yourself with compassion and understanding *"It's okay that I felt upset."*

Use Daily Affirmations

Try these affirmations and use them to replace self criticism or remind yourself to be kind to Number

One.

1. I accept the best and the worst of who I am.
2. Changing is never simple, but it's easier if I stop being hard on myself.
3. My mistakes just show that I'm growing and learning.
4. It's okay to make mistakes and forgive myself.
5. I am free to let go of others' judgments.
6. It's safe for me to show kindness to myself.
7. I deserve compassion, tenderness, and empathy from myself.
8. I release myself with forgiveness from today and move forward with self love to tomorrow.
9. Everyday is a new opportunity. I won't let self doubt or judgment hold me back from the future.
10. I forgive myself and accept my flaws because nobody is perfect.
11. I'm not the first person to have felt this way, and I won't be the last, but I'm growing.

Be motivated to grow from your mistakes, take risks, and reach your full potential.

Mistakes are valuable. However, for them to be of value, you must first see them as a beneficial and critical part of your life that you cannot avoid and must embrace with an open heart and open mind. Who knows, your biggest mistakes could end up turning into your most glorious victories, as long as you are open to learning and growing from the experience.

◆ ◆ ◆

ACTION ITEM: Write down five daily affirmations and repeat one to yourself everyday.

THE PHOENIX: SELF APPRECIATION

I found a thousand reasons not to like myself. Stuck in a rehab facility. Sequestered from everyone that I know and love. Struggling to make sense of the mess I had made of my life. And yet, this small flame continued to burn inside me. I may have been down, but I'm never out. Many things can be said about me, my past transgressions, my public persona, but no one can ever call me a quitter.

Like The Phoenix rising from the flames, I have always clawed my way out of my darkest moments and built myself back up. Time and time again I refused to be written off. Previously, my first step was getting back in the gym, which was truly my sanctuary. The second step was to concoct an extremely detailed, and somewhat believable, account of what happened that caused me to disappear for days from work to tell my employer to hopefully save my livelihood. The lies and deceit while in my addiction had become second nature. It's how I survived. It truly was an exhausting perpetual series of events.

This time felt different. The internal flame that I had come to appreciate and rely on was stronger and burning hotter. This trait I'd often taken for granted was here to pull me up by my bootstraps for the last time. I can't lie, I was proud.

Self appreciation is about turning the kindness you give to others inwards. Instead of blaming yourself for making mistakes, self appreciation is about saying *"thank you"* to yourself for all the things you have done but taken for granted.

The word self appreciation is not a commonly used term. Most people commonly confuse self appreciation with self esteem, but self appreciation is very unlike self esteem.

Self appreciation is the process of appreciating yourself. Appreciating yourself is about being grateful for yourself. You can be thankful that your body is functioning properly, grateful that you are given your natural talents and gifts. You are appreciative of your weaknesses as well.

Self esteem, on the other hand, is a personal evaluation of your self worth. It is a judgment. Esteem is best defined as respect and admiration. If you value yourself as someone who is worthy of respect and admiration, then you will have high self esteem. If you do not, then you have low self esteem. It is just that simple.

Don't wait for others to appreciate or validate you. For example, if you have done an excellent job as a mother, or father, you don't need to wait for others or a special day to be acknowledged for your efforts. Why not appreciate and validate yourself first for your effort?

Most people allow others to determine if we are good enough or not. We let others determine our worth and happiness; however, appreciation does not always come. Just because you put in the time and effort into something, doesn't mean that others will appreciate all that you've done.

So what if no one appreciates what you have done? Does it mean that what you have done is worthless? Are you going to be resentful towards them for not being appreciative?

As opposed to waiting for or seeking or waiting for approval from others, self-appreciation is always a better choice, because it's something that's within our control. People are more likely to appreciate someone who appreciates themselves.

How To Appreciate Yourself:

1. Don't wait for others to validate you

Don't wait for others to appreciate you, you don't

wait till you achieve something great before you appreciate yourself. Do it for yourself now. You do not have to achieve anything special to appreciate yourself.

There are simple things we have which we can be appreciative of. These are things we pay the least attention to when we are distracted and we most likely take for granted. When it comes to appreciation, it's incumbent upon us to see what we do have, as opposed to what we do not have.

Start with your body parts; your eyes, nose, mouth, ears, fingers, and toes. How do you use them in your daily life? What roles do they play? Then, go to your inner organs such as your heart, stomach, and lungs. Can you be thankful for them too?

2. Use kind words towards yourself

Being appreciative for yourself is as simple as using kind words on yourself. Change the way you speak to yourself internally. Think of the language you would use when you are being appreciative towards someone else, then apply the change of language to yourself. Omit words that create judgment and drama. When you forget to do something, instead of berating yourself, try to appreciate all the times when you did remember to do the things you planned on doing? We as humans tend to focus on our mistakes and forget the times when we are doing things right.

Being more aware of your self talk will help you to appreciate yourself more. Remember, there's an opportunity to show appreciation towards yourself when you want to beat yourself up.

3. Keep a gratitude journal

Using a gratitude journal has many benefits. One benefit is to help you discover things which you have taken for granted. Having a fixed schedule to write in your gratitude journal would help remind you to appreciate yourself. Not only does keeping a gratitude journal allow you to review what you are grateful for over the course of your life but it helps you develop the habit of appreciating yourself. Once you have developed and cultivated the habit, you will eventually realize that even if you don't write your journal daily, you will naturally begin to appreciate yourself more. The more you learn to appreciate yourself the more of a habit it will become.

4. Give yourself a gift

Giving yourself a gift is one of the best ways to show yourself appreciation. Gifts can be something material such as new clothes, a new phone, etc. It can also be something simple such as taking a break from work, a walk through nature, getting yourself a massage, manicure, or pedicure. You may be wondering what the difference is between buying yourself something you desire and getting yourself a gift. The difference is the intention and the feeling behind it. Instead of buying something because you want something, you do it from a place of giving and appreciation. You do it because you want to give thanks to yourself.

When you give yourself something, you have to receive too. The act of giving as well as receiving feels amazing. However, when you desire something, you expect to get it. It's more of a feeling of anticipation. The feelings between the two are very different. Give yourself a gift, not get yourself a gift.

5. Be yourself

The best way to appreciate yourself is to simply be yourself. Someone who is truly appreciative of themselves would allow themselves to just be. They fully accept themselves for who they are as a person. Possessing weaknesses is not a big deal to them. They are aware of what they have to offer others and know when to step back. They see no need to hide from others or be someone they are not. They are appreciative and grateful for all that they are given.

How To Develop Mental Resilience

We all can build ourselves into resilient and strong individuals. Here are five ways to become unbreakable and develop mental resilience to gain control over your life.

1. Increase your pain tolerance

If you want to effectively train your mind to become resilient, you need to increase your tolerance for pain. You do this by letting go of how things should be and accept what is. No expectations, and certainly no feeling of entitlement.

It's truly a matter of perspective. When you feel entitled to something or an easier way in life, you are putting yourself in a position whereby your expectations do not have to be met. This dilemma causes hurt and a loss of control.

When you are at peace with the ups and downs, trials as well as the tribulations of life, you are gaining more control over how you ultimately think and feel. Your tolerance to be able to deal with adversity increases since you're more focused on the solution rather than the presence of your pain.

2. Cultivate a powerful support system

There is nothing wrong with being independent, however, trying to handle it all on your own is a terrible idea in the midst of developing emotional resilience. The truth is that we need each other, we need our support network.

A critical part of developing mental resilience is knowing when to ask for help and when lose the ego. There is real strength in admitting that you feel vulnerable and need someone's helping hand. The feeling of love and support is truly the best medicine while dealing with the hardships of life. It's incumbent upon you to decide who you let close to you and who you can trust. It isn't hard to figure this out.

3. Take responsibility for your feelings

Blaming is easy. It takes a weight off your shoulders, it eases the pain and it creates excuses. However, this does not build mental resilience. You need to learn how to take full responsibility for your feelings when someone else hurts them.

There is a big difference between those who are at fault and those who are responsible. For example, your partner cheated on you, broke your heart, and caused you pain. It's your partner's fault; however, it's your responsibility to deal with it. This sounds unfair, but this is the only way you can build your emotional strength on a feeling which scares you the most and that feeling is pain.

4. Learn to be alone

Some of us are afraid of being alone. That's why we may keep the TV on even if we aren't watching it, scroll through our Facebook news feed forty-five times a day or always seeking some company just to maintain the noise. Spending time alone allows you to think clearly, without distractions, and on a much deeper level.

I am not suggesting that you isolate yourself from

others, but time alone, combined with about five or minutes of meditation, will help you in gaining better control of your feelings and overall mental state. It's best to schedule some alone time. Set aside one hour, twice a week just for you, your thoughts and your feelings. If you haven't tried meditation, there are a bevy of videos online which will show you the basics.

5. Love those who hurt you

One of the best ways to let go is by loving those who have hurt us. When you truly let go, and forgive, you are gaining more control over your feelings and your mindset. This is one of the most important aspects of building mental resilience. You take away the power of someone else who gained it through hurting you. When you overcome the feeling of anger as well as the desire for retaliation, the actions of the other person will no longer control you.

Having the right mindset about pain, surrounding yourself with people you can trust and taking full responsibilities for your feelings are truly the basic components of your inner toughness. The best thing about it is that even when you fail, you will manage to recover pretty quickly because you are built this way.

Do not focus on your ego, it's one of the most common reasons which stops you from growing. Have faith and accept the fact that everything in your life has a purpose. It's how you choose to use it which defines who you are.

ACTION ITEMS: Identity your support system. If you don't have a support group you may reach out to the Apex. Achieve Personal Excellence "Fearless Facebook Community"

Second, choose a journal and write your first gratitude entry.

ONWARD, UPWARD: SELF RESPECT

The swag-factor. You wouldn't have recognized me when I dragged myself to the front gates of Delancey Street. I was down fifty pounds and had been up for well over fifty hours. *"Just another crackhead adrift"* I'm sure they thought. Four months into my stay I'm hitting my stride. I gained my weight back, my regular sleep cycle, and my swag-factor was in full swing. The mind crushing *"Games"* were still wearing on me significantly but I began to have a greater appreciation for them.

Emmanuel recognized my thousand mile stare and felt my angst. He and I both knew my time at Delancey Street had run its course. There are many times in life that you outgrow your situation, whether it's your friends, a relationship or a rehab program catering to ex-convicts with no family ties. I had learned all I could. I respected myself, and my recovery, too much to not continually be pushing forward.

Emmanuel was the first one to tell me about the Salvation Army Program. It sounded like a five-star resort. A six month program, with in and out privileges, focused on recovering the mind, body, and spirit from drug and alcohol addiction. It was time to go. It was my growing self respect which sparked me to embark on a new journey with the Salvation Army. However, when I would eventually graduate from this program... I realized I had never really known self respect until that moment.

You may not be aware of this in your everyday life, but how you take care of yourself is crucial to your quality of life. Self respect is quite indicative of how you view yourself. Showing self respect keeps your positive feelings about yourself flowing and growing. Feeling good about yourself and demonstrating self respect are a chicken and egg situation. It can be difficult to tell which comes first. Do positive emotions and thoughts about yourself lead to self respect or is it the other way around? The truth is that they both influence each other. When you diligently practice self respect, you will feel more positive emotions and thoughts about yourself. When you experience more positive emotions and thoughts about yourself, your self respect will come naturally.

There are so many things which you can do to improve your self respect, that once you try, you cannot fail.

Tips To Help You Grow Your Self Respect

There is a great deal of negativity in our world today and this makes it very easy to lose self respect and develop a negative mindset. Although none of us are perfect, we all have characteristics as well as accomplishments which we should respect about ourselves. Self respect fosters our self belief and this is essential if you want to make the most of your life. The following tips will help you to develop a healthy level of self respect.

1. Choose self respect

With change, the first and most important step is to make the commitment to change, and developing self respect is no different. Before you go any further, make the commitment to practice self respect on an everyday basis.

2. Consider your feelings

Your emotions are as important as everyone else's. So if you're uncomfortable, then act on that information. Take your feelings into account in your everyday life as well as into the decisions you make.

Sadly, many people have been conditioned to require the approval of others. When you require the approval of others, you are truly disrespecting yourself by placing the wants, needs, desires, and opinions of others before your own. You are essentially telling yourself that they are more worthy than you.

3. Avoid making self deprecating comments

Such remarks are often used as humor, which can build rapport between people. However, if you're uncertain about whether you treat yourself with the respect you deserve, avoid making them until you're more sure of yourself. Otherwise your self confidence will greatly suffer.

What you say about yourself over and over (whether out loud or subconsciously) becomes what you believe. You must be clear on the boundary between self deprecating humor and genuine self deprecation. If you struggle with a lack of self respect, it is very safe to assume that you are not clear on where those boundaries lie. Should this be the case, you should avoid all self deprecating comments until you have reached a point where your self respect is grounded.

4. Have a journal

A journal is a simple but powerful tool for creating personal change. There are many different ways that you can use a journal but in this instance you are trying to monitor the frequency in which you lack self respect. Write down each time that you disrespect yourself. Make a note as to what was going through your mind and how you were feeling. Over time, as you continue to build a body of work, you will see a pattern for your behavior which you can deal with.

5. Take care of your emotional needs

Self respect is apparent through the things you do to make yourself comfortable, content, and happy. If any relationship constantly makes you feel emotionally upset or out of balance, then it's time to strongly consider doing something about it.

We all have emotional needs and as kind and generous as most people are, you cannot depend on others to ensure that your emotional needs are met. They have their own lives to live. You need to be aware of your own emotional needs and ensure that they are met. Keeping a journal can be very helpful with this.

6. Acknowledge to yourself that you deserve respectful treatment

We allow others to treat us in the manner that we expect to be treated. We essentially teach others how to treat us. If you feel that others are not treating you with respect, you need to question whether you actually expect to get treated with respect. This is the essence of what assertiveness is all about.

This is as simple as it gets, because you're a human being, you deserve to be treated with fundamental human courtesies, which includes respect. Recognize your own value. When you expect to be treated with respect, you will find that this usually happens. When it does not occur, you will find that you become more confident at speaking up and refusing to be treated in a disrespectful manner.

7. Avoid allowing anyone to treat you disrespectfully

Be very clear that you expect to be treated with kindness and care, whether you're interacting with a co-worker, partner, or even your children.

Sometimes, you might think you're giving someone a break by not insisting on being treated well; However, when you allow others to treat you badly, you're neglecting your own self care and enabling them to practice negative interpersonal habits as well. When you allow others to disrespect you, nobody wins.

Warning: To be clear, if standing up for your rights puts you in any immediate danger, it is best to avoid doing so and simply remove yourself from the situation at the first possible opportunity. If necessary, seek help.

8. Behave in ways that show you care

How you conduct yourself sends a strong message to everyone you come into contact with. Taking care of your body, being mindful of the language you use, and refraining from engaging in socially unacceptable behaviors shows that you have a certain measure of respect for yourself.

Take a moment to think of someone you admire and respect. What is it about this person that earns your respect? Strive to emulate this person and you'll be amazed how your self respect will grow.

9. Treat others with respect

In order to treat others with respect, you need to have a clear perception about how to act in respectful ways, Then you can turn those same actions toward yourself. Make demonstrating respect a way of life.

As I mentioned earlier, you ultimately teach others how to treat you. One way you do this is by refusing to allow others to disrespect you. It's equally as important to demonstrate the respectful behavior that you expect by treating others with the utmost of respect. When you treat others with respect, they are likely to follow your lead and act similarly.

As Gandhi once said *"Be the change you wish to see."* So if you want to see more respect, then you must give more respect. Remember, self respect is truly a cornerstone of self confidence.

Life is truly built from the inside out. Before you can create your external world you must be able to create it internally. For example, you must have a clear purpose for your life, and set and visualize effective goals. The same goes for all relationships. If you want to build relationships based on respect then the most important relationship of all must be based on respect. It all starts with your relationship with yourself. Self respect impacts every area of your life. Implement these strategies for practicing self respect in your life, and as you make these practices habitual, you'll automatically begin to treat yourself and others in respectful ways. You'll be amazed at how much your quality of life will increase.

ACTION ITEM: Identify those people in your life who are not giving you the respect you've earned. Have a conversation with them about how you need them to show up for you in your life. If you feel the relationship is beyond saving, remove them from your life.

SALVATION: SELF TRUST

My decision to leave Delancey Street was not an easy one. I was departing from a place which on one hand was causing me severe emotional pain and distress, but on the other hand was a known evil. I knew what to expect and what was expected of me. I went to work each day, I had a bed to sleep in, a roof over my head, and three square meals a day. Taking the leap of faith to walk away from a virtual safety net back onto the streets of San Francisco without any definitive promise of a place to land was the biggest demonstration of self trust I had up until this point.

I trusted myself to not stray from my purpose. Sixth street, the Tenderloin, the despair I had fallen into, was all waiting for me as I took my first step outside the gates. I can't say I didn't entertain a few alternate scenarios. Ones that allowed me to dip my toe into my previous lifestyle, just to reminisce. How much can one dance with the devil hurt?

Fortunately there was a louder voice and it was God, speaking to me through Emmanuel. An angel sent to guide me in the right direction. It is no coincidence that Emmanuel is Hebrew for *"God with us"* used in the bible as a sign that God will protect. Emmanuel believed in me. God believed in me. He trusted me to be true to my word. To not throw away the four months of sobriety I had achieved through blood, sweat, and tears. He trusted me to walk right out of those Delancey Street gates and directly to the front door of the Salvation Army to continue my journey. The journey to self love is a rocky one, and these phases don't always just start within. Sometimes you get a divine intervention to guide you to trusting yourself in ways you never realized you could.

Self trust is best defined as a deep reliance on one's own ability to handle life. Self trust is the mindset of *"Whatever comes my way, I will be able to handle it."* Someone with a high degree of self trust feels safe in relying upon their own mental, emotional, and physical abilities, and there is a deep understanding that life will not overtake them easily.

What Gets In The Way Of Self Trust?

Self abandonment. Habitually going against yourself. Over time, self abandonment results in a lack of self trust, which then bleeds into your ability to trust other people in your life.

If you find yourself constantly struggling to believe that other people actually care about you, or you aren't sure if others have your best interest at heart, you need to recognize that this can all be a function of projection and that you may be the one who isn't caring about yourself, or having your own best interests at heart. If you are kind to yourself then it will be that much easier to trust the kindness of others.

In terms of the root issues of what gets in the way of self trust, there are two major issues.

> 1. *Our truth was made wrong by family, friends, society, or our peer group around us.*
> 2. *We are in the habit of going against what our heart says to us, because our truth is somehow viewed as inconvenient.*

In either case, self trust is reclaimed by rekindling the relationship with ourselves, and treating ourselves as we would our most cherished friend or loved one.

Specific Practices To Boost Self Trust

As with anything that has to do with relationship building,(regardless of whether that relationship is with you or with others) this should be seen as a war of attrition as opposed to a war of annihilation.

So in other words, do as many of these aforementioned things as often as possible, and allow it to grow with time. There is no immediate actionable silver bullet that will help you build a deep sense of self trust overnight. Simply do your best to be compassionate and patient with yourself as you learn to develop your self trust. This process as with anything will take time, but it will truly be worth it.

So without further adieu, here are some exercises that you can practice regularly to develop resilient self trust.

Spend Time With Yourself

Any relationship would struggle to thrive if the people in it didn't spend quality time together, so in the same token, you too must spend quality time with yourself. If your schedule is extremely tight that you don't have any moments of quiet and solitude, then your self trust is likely to suffer.

Do you often go to bed with a racing mind? Thoughts coming at you from every angle, vying and begging for your attention? Then perhaps you may be long overdue for some quality *"me-time."* You can set the foundation for improved self trust with taking advantage of your *"me-time."*

Be In Dialogue With Yourself

Truly, anything that causes you to slow down and

observe your own mind is highly beneficial. Journal. Sit and meditate. Lie down on your bed and just breathe for awhile and see what comes up. For a more proactive approach, you can look inwards and ask yourself questions such as, *"How have I have been feeling lately?"*, *"Is there anything that I need to do to honor myself more fully?"*, or *"What does my heart need more of?"*

Ask these questions, receive the answers, then act upon what your inner wisdom offers you. Your body, heart, and mind already know what you need. It simply needs you to slow down long enough and take a step back so that you can hear the messages being sent your way.

Be Willing To Take Risks In Your Life

One of the most potent ways that we can build more self-trust is by regularly challenging and pushing ourselves. Whether or not we succeed in accomplishing the objective, the mere act of giving ourselves the challenge grows our self-esteem and self-trust because it sends the message that we are someone who is worthy enough to be challenged with difficult things in the first place.

So ask out that attractive person you have a crush on. Initiate that tough conversation with someone who you have been meaning to clear the air with. Go after that job you want. Push yourself in your physical fitness goals. Move forward in your life and claim what you want.

It's these types of actions that ultimately build self trust. You simply have to be willing to accept the challenge, and do your best.

Set Realistic Goals

Speaking to the opposite side of the previous spectrum listed above, you need to have enough compassion for yourself to set sane enough goals that you aren't just constantly whipping yourself through life.

Push yourself, yes, but also be kind to yourself.

Some of the most productive and successful people throughout history, were also experts at having balanced lives with ample leisure time. For example, did you know that Charles Dickens had a strict schedule of writing for five hours, followed by a daily three hour walk? What a true beast! Who needs to brag about their sixteen hour work day on social media when there's beautiful nature to embrace!

Reward Yourself

Whether you're rewarding yourself for one of your goals being achieved, or you're giving yourself a reward because you deserve nice things once in a while, rewarding ourselves is a necessary habit to get into.

I used to be guilty of not doing this.

In the first seven years of building up my business, I would work for 8-12 hours a day, seven days a week, and I would constantly dangle the carrot in front of myself of, "When I hit this goalpost, then I'll reward myself with XYZ!" But I never did. I would hit the goal, and then I'd immediately move the goal post further. And as a result, my heart began to distrust me. I was driving myself unnecessarily and never giving myself a chance to rest.

Think of this as being similar to if you were on a road trip, and your kids are in the back seat and you keep telling them that you're going to stop and get some delicious food soon, but then you never fulfill your promise.

One of two things would happen: 1. The kids would quickly stop believing you because you don't fulfill your promises, and 2. The kids would eventually starve.

Now to bring it back to the self trust comparison, this is exactly what happens when we do not slow down to give ourselves ample rest, and reward ourselves for a job well done. First, our mind stops believing us (and starts sending us increasingly loud indicators of stress until we are forced to listen), and then our connection to ourselves begins to die and we become increasingly numb and despondent.

This strategy known as *"trying to get blood from a*

stone" doesn't work long-term. You must be kind to yourself. Anything short of that will bite you in the rear sooner than later in the end.

Practice Regular Self Care

Just as you would probably struggle to feel deeply connected to an intimate partner that doesn't treat you well, it's imperative that you take good care of yourself in your life. A stand up comedian, I recently saw made the observation that "*Self care is so stressful because it never ends!*"

Self care doesn't have to be complicated. A healthy diet full of nutrient dense foods, a regular bedtime, rest, relaxation, and ample time for hobbies, friends, and play. If you do each of these things, most of the time, it's truly as simple as that.

Work Out Your Problems On Your Own

If you have the sense that you are too quick to go to others for help and that it would be in your best interest to sit with yourself for a moment longer, then this point is truly for you.

An essential element of self trust is knowing that you can handle whatever comes your way. You can prove this to yourself in real time by looking internally for the answers to your problems, more often than not.

Leaning on people is okay as we are a social species

and need each other to survive. However, if you are the type of person who frequently outsources your important life decisions to a panel of your peers, then you would be better off sorting out your own problems.

Swing the pendulum and try it out for a few weeks, and see how it feels. You may enjoy it, and feel a lot more empowered as an individual.

Work Out Your Problems By Asking For Help

Conversely, if you are the type of person who has a hard time asking for any help and you are prone to solving your problems on your own, then you would be better served by intentionally leaning on others more often than you do.

Ask for help. Lean on your friends. Let your family be there for you. Accept the love and support that is around you. The people that you love, love you back and are willing to find a way to support you. So allow them to.

Respect Your Opinion As Much As You Respect The Opinion Of Others (If Not More)

If you're looking to cultivate self trust, there's a good chance that for much of your life you haven't had much weight to the truths that come to you from within. While the mind and ego are often the Pandora's box for nonsense, you want to be sure that any messages that are coming to you from your intuition and heart are being acknowledged.

The single greatest tool that I can give you to know whether something is coming from your ego or from your gut are these examples:
Let's say you're trying to make a decision, and you could go one of two ways. Hold one answer in your mind and see how your body responds. If your gut, stomach, or heart tenses up and you feel trapped, sick, or anxious, then that's likely not the way to go. On the flip side, if you think of the answer and your gut, heart, or body releases, then that is most likely the way you need to go.

This stuff can be somewhat nuanced (Is your gut releasing because it's the right path to choose, or because going with that option absolves you of responsibility or allows you to not have to face into some challenging thing that you should lean into?) but the more you ask these questions, the easier the answers come with time.

Gather Evidence Of Times That Your Decisions Went Well For You

There's a chance that you have lacked self trust in the past because you've been overly in the habit of forgetting the times that trusting yourself went well, and magnifying the times that trusting yourself went poorly.

Negativity bias is real and we all do this to some

extent. A hundred people say something nice to you and one person gives you a nasty criticism that hits too close to home, and you bask in the negative feedback.

Instead, tip the scale in the other direction by making a list of all the times you practiced self trust and the result was a unilateral success for you.

Avoid People Who Shame Or Belittle Your Truth

Another way that we further distance ourselves from a strong sense of self trust is by surrounding ourselves with people who belittle or shame our truths. First off, if this is you, I truly feel for you, because being made to feel crazy, wrong, or stupid for your heart's truth is nothing short of horrendous. Secondly, change this.

Having our truth feel wrong can feel like our inner child showing it's finger paintings to a trusted guardian and having that guardian laugh at it.

If you feel a lack of support from the group of people that you're surrounded with, it's incumbent upon you to either discontinue a relationship with those people, or if that isn't possible, start to minimize time with them and or refrain from discussing certain things with those people.

These situations are dynamic and multifaceted... so I cannot cover every angle of what's happening for you in this book.

Long story short, be around people that support you and lift you up. Invest in those relationships and treat them like the gold. In my heavily biased opinion, there's nothing more important than finding your support group of people, loving them hard, and letting them influence you for the better. With all that I have and all that I've achieved for my relatively young life, my close friends are the greatest part of my life, by a large margin.

Continue To Build Self Trust, And Support Your Process With Self Compassion

It's important to understand that cultivating self-trust is a lifelong process. It is often a tricky balance to know which part of yourself you are listening to and honoring, but it does get easier with time. Lean towards challenging things, grow your self esteem through your actions, and continue to embrace life experiences and get the feedback of where your decisions lead you.

In time, you won't need to set aside a full hour or more to compel your heart to give you breadcrumbs of the truth, as it will come freely and clearly. You will get there with time and time is what you have. Don't worry about hacking your way through this stuff overnight.

And, especially if you've made it this far into the book and all the way to the end of it, I believe in you, and I have no doubt you'll get there in your own way.

◆ ◆ ◆

ACTION ITEM: Schedule one hour each week for yourself. Put it into your calendar. Use this time to journal, meditate, read, or just be with yourself. However you spend it is up to you. Just don't cancel this appointment with yourself.

APEX: SELF PERMISSION

The streets have their own set of rules. You must know and follow them to survive. You're often required to create and project a certain persona, one of complete confidence coupled with zero personal responsibility. I had always projected an aura of confidence, at times crossing over into arrogance. However, it was a mask. The pain and inadequacies I felt inside were constantly threatening to overflow. Each time I gained the slightest bit of traction in my personal life or a potential career, I unintentionally sabotaged myself. Wholly eradicating my previous efforts. *What was I afraid of? Why wasn't I worthy of success?* Perhaps I just wasn't good enough.

Of course negative self talk pops up throughout every experience in our lives, and my transition into life at the Salvation Army, a minimally restrictive rehab program, was no different. After the initial thirty day *"detox"* phase, I had more freedom to move around. This afforded me an opportunity to really ingratiate myself with the staff and fellow residents of the program. I found that natural leader within myself that had been hiding and broken for many years. It could have been my 6'4" stature and 270 pound build but my cohort started looking up to me for guidance and advice. Coming from Delancey Street with four months of sobriety under my belt, gave me some experience and wisdom I could impart.

I quickly rose through the ranks, given more and more responsibility. This culminated in me being appointed Dorm Leader for the remainder of my stay. A position I did not take lightly. I gave myself permission to not only succeed, but to truly excel in that role. I noticed a huge change in my own demeanor as I treated everyone in my dorm with respect and dignity, even when they were not reciprocating. I approached them as men, as individuals, and as equals to collaborate our efforts to change our lives. From the tidiness of our dorm, to the integrity of our step work. I had hit my stride that would carry me through the coming months. Spoiler alert! This time I didn't sabotage myself. I gave myself permission.

You and I are hard wired to seek permission. As children, we needed permission from parents, teachers and elders. In adulthood, we seek permission from our bosses and authorities. Our mind is conditioned to ask for permission. But in order to unlock your full potential, you have to learn to give yourself permission and assume ownership of your life.

When you take complete ownership of your life, you are in charge of your life experiences. There is absolutely no room for blame or excuses. Don't place the keys to your life in the hands of other people nor become the prison guard. You'll completely forget that you have the key to unlock the full potential of your life.

Well, I'm here to remind you of the permissions that you must give yourself.

You Must Give Yourself The Permission To Succeed

You are capable of accomplishing amazing things. However, first you must allow yourself to be successful. Some people are truly afraid of success. Some people believe that being successful means making a lot of money or being greedy. This kind mental rhetoric has to leave your mind completely.

Success is truly subjective, always remember that. You have the power to define your own criteria and prerequisites for success. It could be being a good husband or wife, having a positive attitude at the end of the day, having the freedom to travel the world or taking small steps towards your goal.

No matter what success means to you, you have to own it and live up to it. Forget about what society's definition of what success is. Write down your own definition and move towards that direction. In order to make success a habit, set more behavior based goals as opposed to outcome based goals. Here's an example, if you want to lose weight, you must define success by making the right food choices instead of the number on the scale. If you continue to succeed at the behavior based goals and move in the right direction, the outcome soon will follow.

So start now! It does not matter how small the first step is and it doesn't matter how slow the progress is. By default, life has no meaning, however; if you continue to strive to achieve personal excellence, you can give your life a purpose. A purpose driven life.

Give Yourself Permission To Fail

Failure is truly a form of learning. Failure is not a prerequisite for success but it helps to amplify the success. In making mistakes, you not only learn, but you undoubtedly build a character that renovates every other area of your life. Your will mindset will change. You understand and embrace success more because of the effort you put towards it.

If you learn to let go of the fear of failure, you will not be afraid to discover the possibilities of your life. You will become **FEARLESS**, because you understand that making mistakes accelerates your learning as well as your results in growth. Allow yourself to be imperfect. Put your product or craft out in public and embrace the feedback.

All the magazines and social media feeds show us the faces of successful people. It seems as though they are perfect people, living a perfect life with no flaws. But in reality, they are just like you and me. They continue learning from failures.

In a world where success is heavily preached, don't be afraid to look like a failure. Failure is not a scar on your self esteem. It's truly a battle scar you can be proud of. This quote from George Bernard Shaw says it all: *"A life spent making mistakes is not only more honorable, but more useful than a life spent doing nothing."*

Give Yourself Permission To Be Yourself

When we fake our identity, we try to live up to the fake version we show to the world. It's incredibly stressful to live up to people's expectation of who they think you should be. On the flip side, if you be true to yourself, you will attract the right kind of people in your life and you won't have to put time and energy into displaying a fake version of yourself. The very first step to being yourself is to fully accept yourself. This means not only accepting the good but also accepting the flaws that are within you.

The reason why some people put on a mask is that it is in our instinct to get accepted into communities. We could only survive if we were part of a group. The outcasts were rejected and they could not live very long. But in today's world, when you have access to a bevy of people, you need not to fear people's rejection. You can always find like minded people if you express yourself just as you are.

So release all of the emotional baggage, forgive yourself, and move on, because all you truly have is today. You have the opportunity to define your future and it will only be great if you learn to stop hurting yourself with the pain of the past.

From this day moving forward, you can control who you want to be. Define your values, set goals, follow your passion, and more importantly, stay true to yourself. Don't be afraid to change. Raise your standards and if you have to, relinquish your past identity and change the people around you.

Learn to say no to the people or experiences that do not appeal to you. Life is far too short to be fake or inauthentic.

"To be yourself in a world that is constantly trying to make you something else is the greatest accomplishment." Ralph Waldo Emerson

"Be yourself, everyone else is already taken" Oscar Wilde

Give Yourself Permission To Be Happy

You truly deserve to be happy. You don't have to wait for the next paycheck, vacation, or a soulmate to be happy. Many times, we spend our lives thinking about the time in future when we will be happy. Even after getting what we want, we adapt to the gifts in our life. It's perfectly okay to desire more success but first, you must learn to be happy with what you have. Count your blessings.

Happiness is a skill. If you can't be happy today, you won't be happy tomorrow. In order to cultivate the happiness skill, you can start by practicing gratitude and mindfulness. Take a break from the rigors of life and do things that you find fun or relaxing. You don't have to pretend to enjoy the activities that other people might like.

Write a bucket list of the life experiences that you want to have and live those experiences. Nobody should give you the permission to live your life the way you want. Another great way to be happy is to help others. Kindness not only makes the world a better place, it allows you to see past the problems you have in your life.

Give Yourself Permission To Feel Your Emotions

No matter how much you try to avoid negative emotions such as anger, frustration, sadness, jealousy, etc. You will feel them at times during your life. You don't have to feel bad about feeling bad because it's okay to feel that way. It's our human nature to feel emotions. Instead of resisting these emotions, try observing them when they arrive. When you acknowledge them and treat them as a guest, they will leave sooner than you expect them to stay in your mind.

Emotions are beautiful. They help us deal with hard situations. If you become more aware of your emotions, soon you will return to your default positive state if you continue to practice the skill of being a happy person. Don't allow negative emotions to define you. Define yourself as a happy person and treat negative emotions as something you feel temporarily.

The key to your best life is in your hands. Unlock the life you deserve to live, because your life does in fact matter. Give yourself permission to succeed, fail, be yourself, be happy and feel emotional to achieve your full potential and truly live a fulfilled life.

ACTION ITEM: Identify the things in your life you need to give yourself permission to do. Take one small step to do them.

THE GRADUATION: RECEIVE THE BLESSINGS

My hand was trembling with excitement as I sat down to write my commencement speech. *How do you summarize twelve years of substance and alcohol abuse?* The ups, the downs, the rock bottom that changed your life forever, and the incredibly difficult journey which followed. I had to reflect. I needed to calm my mind and consider my accomplishment. Nothing up to this point in my life mattered more than my sobriety. I had truly earned it.

I noticed that since I had changed my mindset to one of abundance and intention, the dreams and paths I had for myself were unfolding before my eyes. I reenrolled into school to work towards earning my Master's Degree. I was able to move back to my apartment in the neighborhood I loved.

Most importantly, I picked up where I left off with Apex. Achieve Personal Excellence, my raison d'etre (*reason for being*). The old adage, *"Do something you love and you'll never work a day in your life"* couldn't be more true for me and my love affair with helping people to achieve personal excellence through health, wellness, education, and spirituality. I had returned home.

It was definitely not a solo journey; I had much help along the way. However, I needed to open my heart to receive the message, to receive the assistance, and to ultimately, receive the blessings.

Everything in life is in a flow. Energy is constantly flowing to us and through us, so when it comes to opening the door to receiving more love, more blessings, more happiness, more creativity and more life affirming abundance, there are a couple of things we need to do first to get out of our own way.

Let Go Of Fear

Have you ever found yourself so afraid of failure, so panic-stricken about potential loss, or not living up to expectations, that you're spinning your wheels on success? Do you find yourself running away from opportunity or saying no to more shimmering brilliance in your life because you think you're undeserving or *"not quite there yet?"*

Are you more loyal to your fears than you are to

your dreams? It's a strong question to ask yourself, and as you begin to sharpen your tools and start being open to more abundance in your life, there's no doubt that fear will rear its ugly head. Fear is natural as well as uncomfortable and it can suck the life out of you (*if you allow it to*) however, it can also be totally transformative.

In order to fully open yourself up to receiving all the glorious gifts the Universe has on offer, you must call your fear out. Call it out and then stamp it out. When you refuse to be small, and take a risk by opening yourself up, with the intention to receive more in your life, what you are in truth doing, is nourishing the part of you that magnetizes the good stuff. Energy is energy and by stepping out in good faith as opposed to backing down from your dreams, you raise the veil on a fear driven existence. That tired, played out *"scarcity"* mindset goes right out the window, and you realize that there always has been and always will be enough for everyone.

Give Freely

Load up on love and free it. Give praise that makes someone's day, sprinkle joy with reckless abandon, show that you're genuinely interested, offer your time. You'll feel fulfilled, happier and more deeply satisfied with your life than ever before, and the good news is, while you're basking in the sweet sunshine of selfless service, you're actually enlarging that space within you. This is where the abundance you have opened yourself up to will be able to flow with ease and alacrity.

Get Clear On Exactly What You Want And Ask For It

Clarity is like a jolt of electricity for the soul. When you become clear about what you want more of (*as well as want you don't want*) life will always rise up to meet you in that place of exquisite knowing. It's a wonderful cycle and the good news is that getting there is pretty simple.

It goes something like this:

Step 1:
Proclaim your dreams and desires. Write them down, create a vision board, tape them to your mirror or refrigerator, put them in your purse or wallet.

Step 2:
Immerse yourself in your desires daily. Visualize them, see yourself there, FEEL YOUR DESIRES. (*this is the shrewd part where your every day thoughts shift to support them*) It's important to know that where the mind goes, energy flows and all the things that are in sync with those bold dreams or things you want more of in your life will start being sent your way.

Clarity truly opens the floodgates to affluence in all areas of your life. The right people will show up just when you need them, that awesome new client comes along just as you let go of the one that has been draining your joy, the money you need flows in and everything elevates.

Receive

What do you deserve? A simple question, yes, but a very complex (*and revealing*) one. Right off the bat, I feel that the majority of us would say we deserve to live happy, comfortable, and fulfilling lives, but (*and there's a but*) oftentimes there is something going on at a much deeper level that's in a direct conflict with that statement, pulling us out of alignment.

On a smaller scale, that could mean following up a compliment from a friend with a negative response *"No way, I look terrible!"* or on a larger scale, that could mean devaluing your work or staying in an emotionally abusive relationship. The thing is though, the most important part of the process when it comes to ushering in the spectacular abundance you say you want is knowing, trusting, and believing that you do in fact, deserve to receive it.

Put this in your heart, you have an unlimited capacity to receive. It is perfectly okay to receive abundantly. When it comes to others, allow them the pleasure of giving. Acknowledge kind gestures and believe you're worthy of praise. When it comes to yourself, practice being an excellent receiver by showing deep and humble gratitude for what you already have.

A **scarcity mindset** is based on the belief that everything is limited. However, recognizing fear and making the decision to dive in regardless, will work wonders on releasing your positive energy. The result is that you'll delve further into life, and replace those limiting beliefs of fear that have been keeping you stagnated for so long with a healthy sense of curiosity.

Ideally, it's like waving a gigantic flag with big, bold letters saying...

"I'm ready for more. Show me."

ACTION ITEM: Get clear on EXACTLY what you want and go after it.

REFLECTION

You might be wondering how my father received my apology. Sometimes in life there are things that are beyond your control. We can spend our time agonizing over these wounds, or we can focus on the love which is within our means to heal them. My father has not responded.

In my treatment, I uncovered several open wounds from my childhood. My relationship with both my mother and father were among the deepest. I will continue to make strides and work diligently to repair those bonds.

As for my guide, the voice of God, Emmanuel, I never saw him again. In Delancey Street, I confided in him that when this was all over, when I had come out of rehab on the other side, I would write a book and put him in it. However, I did not know the impact he had had on my life at the time, much less how compelled I would be to describe our paths intersecting in my journey to self love.

I attempted to reunite with him last December, (2019) when I heard he was working one of the many Delancey Street Christmas tree lots in San Francisco. To say I was excited to see him was nothing short of an understatement. I rode the bus in immense anticipation, running through all the things I wanted to tell him. Unfortunately, as I mentioned above, some things are just beyond our grasp. Emmanuel had left the program days before and his whereabouts are unknown. I hope he can reflect back upon our conversations as I do, and let them guide him back to salvation.

Self love has been a lifelong journey for me and I realize that, like my sobriety, it is something that has to be maintained. I realized that if you truly love yourself, you don't put yourself in precarious situations nor do you indulge in damaging vices such as drugs and alcohol or even negative self talk.

As you go out in the world today, make it your mission to get crystal clear about what you want out of life. Kick fear to the curb, create space for abundance to flow in and keep asking for more. The Universe is awaiting you to say yes.

Let the words of the Serenity Prayer resonate with you on your journey to self love.

> *"God grant me the serenity, to accept the things I cannot change... the courage to change the things I can, and the wisdom to know the difference."* Amen.

ABOUT THE AUTHOR

Stephen Ukaoma

Stephen Ukaoma is a Certified Life Coach, Motivational Writer, and now, Published Author. After battling and overcoming a twelve year addiction to drugs and alcohol, he came out on the other side with a renewed sense of purpose: to help others Achieve Personal Excellence. He began this mission with the formation of Apex. in 2015, and has been running full steam ahead ever since. He recently relocated to San Francisco in pursuit of his higher education degree in Psychology.

www.ingramcontent.com/pod-product-compliance
Lightning Source LLC
Chambersburg PA
CBHW051900130726
47987CB00002B/910